THE CHURCH'S COMMON TREASURE

THE ROMAN MISSAL ✠ THIRD EDITION

COMMITTEE ON COMMUNICATIONS
UNITED STATES CONFERENCE OF CATHOLIC BISHOPS

UNITED STATES CONFERENCE OF CATHOLIC BISHOPS
WASHINGTON, D.C.

The document *The Church's Common Treasure: The Roman Missal, Third Edition* was developed as a resource by the Committee on Communications of the United States Conference of Catholic Bishops (USCCB). It was reviewed by the committee chairman, Bishop Gabino Zavala, and has been authorized for publication by the undersigned.

Msgr. David J. Malloy, STD
General Secretary, USCCB

First printing, December 2010

ISBN 978-1-60137-158-4

Contents

Foreword

The implementation of the English translation of the *Roman Missal, Third Edition* raises many questions for English-speaking Catholics in the United States. Why do we need a new translation? How will it be different? How will this translation affect lay ministers and liturgical musicians? Just who are these new saints in this edition of the Missal? Why is the *Roman Missal* so important?

None of these questions has a short, simple answer. Scholarly reports and analyses often raise more questions than they answer for the average Catholic. That is why this short volume tackles these questions from the perspective of journalists, who regularly take large, complex issues and break them down into succinct, easy-to-read stories.

Here you will find eleven essays by members of the Catholic press, exploring the history and purpose of the *Roman Missal* and this new translation. These writers discuss how the translation will affect lay ministers and people in the pew. They shed light on the spiritual significance of the Mass in the life of Catholics. They unearth some of the riches that the *Roman Missal* offers the church.

As one writer observes, the *Roman Missal* is the church's common treasure. My hope and prayer is that this volume helps Catholics better appreciate it.

+ Gabino Zavala

Bishop Gabino Zavala
Chairman, Committee on Communications
United States Conference of Catholic Bishops

The *Roman Missal*:
The Church's Common Treasure

Lynn S. Williams

The new English translation of the *Roman Missal,* the official manual for the Roman Catholic Mass, has been approved, and soon familiar prayers and responses said in churches around the English-speaking world will change. Priests will follow newly translated instructions. Prayers used throughout the Mass and some responses of the congregation will change. Sacred chants and music used in worship will also be updated.

The English translation received *recognitio,* or approval, from the Vatican in April of 2010. Though no timetable for implementation has been announced, it's generally believed the new translation will be used starting Advent 2011. It will be the most significant change to the Mass in over 40 years.

An occasion like this raises the question: Why is the *Roman Missal* so important?

"The *Roman Missal* is a common treasure," says Msgr. Anthony Sherman, executive director at USCCB Secretariat of Divine Worship. "It is the book that provides us with prayer text. It serves as a point of unity that keeps us all together, presenting the prayers that are used around the world, in many languages, during universal feasts or holy days."

Latin is the core text of the *Roman Missal,* evolving from oral tradition to written words. During the 15th century, in the era of the first printing press, the earliest book called *Missale Romanum* appeared. After the Council of Trent in 1570, Pope Pius V issued the edition that set the premier standard of uniformity used by celebrants of the Catholic faith.

Eight former popes issued new editions between 1604 and 2002, and each maintained a consistent style of worship for prayer in the Roman rite. Over time, additional Masses, prayers and revised rubrics (instructions) used to celebrate the Mass were added. The need for vernacular translations of the *Roman Missal* arose after the Second Vatican Council, and the present English translation of the Mass, which dates back to the 1970s, follows the Vatican's guidelines of that time, which favored translations that were easy to understand in the vernacular.

When Pope John Paul II issued the third edition of the *Roman Missal* in 2002, a new English translation was required. Since the new English translation is guided by the 2001 Vatican document *Liturgiam Authenticam,* it presents a more literal translation of Latin wording and sentence structure than is used in the current translation.

"The current translations are centered more on the community than the divine," says Father Paul Turner, a parish pastor in the Diocese of Kansas City-St. Joseph, Missouri, and author of *Let Us Pray: A Guide to the Rubrics of Sunday Mass.* "They were somewhat inattentive to inclusive language, and lacked some theological depth and musicality. The first translations condensed some of the content of the prayers. The new translation improves that," he says.

"This is not a new Mass," says Michael McMahon, president of the National Association of Pastoral Musicians, adding that with a new translation, "one of the opportunities we have is to look at the parts of the Mass that should be sung" in the dialogue between the priest and the people and integrate them. One of the challenges of introducing a newly translated missal is retraining priests to lead Mass. Downloadable recordings for priests who don't read music are being produced and distributed free, online. Major publishers will release material on compact discs.

The *Roman Missal* itself is the primary source of training and instruction for the new translation. It displays rubrics, sentences printed in red that instruct a priest on what to say and do, how and when to gesture, and when to sing the common prayers in The Order of Mass. It provides instructions that guide the celebrant in leading the liturgy and the people assembled in ritual response for each occasion of Mass.

It also dictates the words used by a priest during the Mass, which with the new translation will reflect a more formal style than past translations.

"It will sound much more like Latin," says Father Turner.

"*The Roman Missal* puts us into a tradition of prayer and creates a historical awareness in the roots of where we are now," says Msgr. Sherman. "When you study the background of these prayers, you become united" with the perpetual mission of the church.

The *Roman Missal*:
The Challenges of Change

Beth Dotson Brown

Change is often accompanied by fear that challenges priests in the United States when preparing to use the new translation of the *Roman Missal.* Yet, amidst the newness of the prayers there are also opportunities that church leaders say can guide congregations to a richer liturgical and spiritual life.

"I think we've always had an opportunity for a deeper prayer, but I do think the translation is getting more nuance out of the text than we've had before," says Father Paul Turner, an author, lecturer and pastor in Missouri. "So we've got some deeper possibilities for catechesis and for spirituality with this translation."

That deeper appreciation of the liturgy begins with the priest who will lead the people in using the missal. Msgr. Anthony Sherman, executive director of the Secretariat of Divine Worship at the U.S. Conference of Catholic Bishops (USCCB), sees this as an opportunity for priests to further develop their own spiritual lives so they can ignite the faith of the congregation.

"The basic context of the eucharistic prayers is the same, therefore it's an opportunity for priests . . . to take a look at some of the background material," he says, noting that the USCCB Web site has numerous resource materials posted.

He observes that in order for the missal to be successfully implemented, "the priest needs to be able to pray each prayer. And the only way one can approach this in a more prayerful manner is to educate oneself on the background of the prayers, theological concepts contained in the prayer, because then you can more intelligently and convincingly proclaim them for the people."

Father Turner agrees. "Our greatest challenge is to get inside those and make them sound like our prayer and not just the missal's prayer," he says. "We need to spend time with the prayer ourselves, meditating on them and figuring out more deeply what they mean, imagining some context in our own lives that can make this prayer more authentic for us."

Although priests have always tried to do this, the new language in the translation presents them with possible stumbling blocks they will need to work through.

Because the new translation is truer to the Latin syntax, the sentences are sometimes long and grammatically complex. There are also vocabulary changes. Msgr. Sherman suggests priests read over the text to learn the best way to proclaim them. The more comfortable the priest is with these changes, the easier it will be for the congregation to learn them.

Although new missals will not be available until a year after the final translation is approved, it is not too early for priests to begin preparing their congregations as well. Msgr. Sherman suggests printing some of the new text in the church bulletin so people will begin to understand it. He also encourages parishes to explain why the new translation was needed and how it was created.

"The books we use to celebrate are at the center of our liturgical life," Msgr. Sherman says. "That's what binds us all together. Every single country in the world has that text as the basis for the translation." Therefore, every country will be using a new translation.

The process of translation has been long and difficult, and has included the participation of a number of people, something Father Turner feels is important for those in the U.S. church to know. Living in a democracy, he says, "I think there's some natural resistance when something comes to us from the top down."

If priests can peacefully introduce the new texts to their congregations, it can have great benefits. The new edition of the *Roman Missal* also has special items that Catholics can look forward to. For instance, one reason the new missal was needed was that Pope John Paul II canonized a great number of saints. The new missal will include texts to celebrate these saints.

"These prayers will have to work on us in our psyche and our prayer life for a number of years before we capture the whole meaning," says Msgr. Sherman. "I think we're also going to be on the verge of everyone in the church being able to appreciate these prayers in a way that we never did in the past."

Gained in Translation:
The Challenges of the *Roman Missal*

Peter Feuerherd

A translator is a traitor.

Father Paul Turner, a priest of the Diocese of Kansas City-St. Joseph, knows the saying as an inside joke among those who move words, phrases and meanings from one language to another. He points out that the joke works better in Italian, where the words for traitor and translator are almost the same.

But in any language the phrase points to a greater truth, says Father Turner, a Latin scholar who worked for the International Commission on English in the Liturgy (ICEL), which developed the translation of the new *Roman Missal*.

"Anytime you translate you are doing your best. But it is nearly impossible to capture all the nuances and bring them into a new language," he says.

At the ICEL commission meetings Father Turner served as a recorder of the proceedings held by 11 bishops from the English-speaking world. Led by Bishop Arthur Roche of Leeds, England, the group reviewed liturgical translations. Along with other scholars, Father Turner, who is also pastor of St. Muchin Church in Cameron, Mo., could raise points about meaning and grammar, but only the bishops voted on the actual approvals.

Sometimes proposed suggestions were inserted into the revised texts; other times suggestions failed to win approval. The group, says Father Turner, was determined that the original Latin of the liturgical texts was faithfully rendered into English as much as possible.

"We want the liturgy to be understood," he says. "But those who pray it have to know that it is the prayer being brought to us by the tradition." The result, for American Catholics who first encounter the missal, will take some adjustment.

The current translation focuses on rendering the texts understandable to modern English speakers, while the new translation will focus more on keeping the nuances in the original Latin. The result will be the use of some phrases and words that are not normally a part of everyday English discourse.

"It's not that the translation we have is wrong or heretical. But what we gained in fluidity (in English) we lost in nuance (from the Latin)," says Father Turner.

For example: The new translation uses the word "ineffable" to describe the power of God. Webster's defines the word as anything "incapable of being expressed in words." While not a part of daily English speech—although Father Turner notes he saw the word in a recent edition of *Newsweek*—"it's a great word when you talk about the mystery of God. It is a word that means we are speechless before God." When taken in context, he says, English speakers will become familiar with it for a description of a mysterious quality of God.

Other examples: In the creed of the new missal, the old translation read that Jesus was "one in being" with the Father. The new translation will describe this relationship as "consubstantial," an English word as close to the original Latin meaning as possible.

"It's an unusual word. But the relationship between Jesus and the Father is unusual and needs a unique word," says Father Turner, who adds that ancient church councils attempted to define this relationship in as precise a way as possible, and modern English speakers should have the benefit of those insights.

Each Sunday American Catholics routinely recite the creed, in which Jesus is described as "born of the Virgin." That phrase, says Father Turner, fails to capture the full nature of Jesus. "Incarnate," the word used in the new translation, is intended to emphasize that at Jesus' conception the divine was present.

It may sound strange at first but, says Father Turner, English-speaking Christians through the ages have recited the Lord's Prayer, with its famous phrase, "hallowed be thy name." The word "hallowed" is rarely used in English anymore, but English speakers reciting the Lord's Prayer easily recognize it in that context. The same should hold true for the terminology in the new missal, says Father Turner.

The ultimate goal will be English-speaking Catholics reciting prayers that more precisely render their original Latin meanings, making the traitor in translation as unobtrusive as possible.

The New Translation Is a Plus for Catholics

James Breig

Microsoft Vista and "New Coke" have proven that not every change is for the better. Furthermore, when change comes to important elements of life, it is often resisted with the cry of "we never did it that way before."

However, experts who are enthusiastic about the changes to the *Roman Missal*—the book that contains the prayers for the Mass—think the alterations are improvements that will lead to a deeper spiritual experience.

"Because a new edition of the Latin *Roman Missal* was issued in 2002, it is necessary for all the countries of the world to translate this missal into the vernacular," says Msgr. Anthony Sherman, executive director of the U.S. Conference of Catholic Bishops Secretariat of Divine Worship, in explaining why the changes are being made.

But translation is not something easy to accomplish, concedes Msgr. Kevin Irwin, dean of the School of Theology and Religious Studies at The Catholic University of America in Washington. "We all bring our own prejudices and ideas to translation," he says. "It is hoped that the new texts will be more accurate so that our faith and our statements of faith are reliable."

Msgr. Irwin says changes to the *Roman Missal* are rare. "The previous *Roman Missal* (in Latin) was published in 1570, with minor adjustments [being made] in editions through 1962," he says. "After the Second Vatican Council, the new [*Roman Missal*] was published in 1970, followed by a 1975 edition with minor adjustments and then the third edition in 2002 with additional prayers for new saints' feasts, etc."

Father Paul Turner of the Diocese of Kansas City-St. Joseph in Missouri elaborated on the latter point, saying that the missal "includes additional saints' days that are now on the calendar, as well as some Masses for other circumstances. In addition, the rubrics in Holy Week have many small emendations."

What makes the translation of the 2002 edition of the *Roman Missal* different is that it is carried out under the latest Vatican guidelines for translating the Mass into vernacular languages. This new guideline, *Liturgiam Authenticam,* published in 2001, urges a stronger adherence to Latin wording and structure than earlier directives. The results have led to some concern, voiced even by bishops, that the new English translations of the missal are not user-friendly. The vast majority of God's people in the assembly are not familiar with words 'ineffable,' 'consubstantial' and 'inviolate.'"

Msgr. Sherman counters that "in the United States today, people are almost daily learning new vocabulary, and sometimes it is quite technical. The words in our liturgical prayers can afford celebrants the opportunity to reflect on the broader context of those words and so lead the faithful in a deeper understanding of the beliefs being explained."

He grants that "the new translation is not perfect because, in a certain sense, no translation can be perfect. The differences of opinion on the translation will be wide. At some future date, the Holy See may substitute a different prayer for what we now have. On the other hand, some have already expressed the opinion that this translation sometimes captures with a greater eloquence the content of the particular prayers."

Msgr. Irwin says that the church uses technical words in its vocabulary sometimes because those words capture concepts of the faith that would not be easy to understand without using a lot of other words. "For example, since the 13th century, we have used the term 'transubstantiation' to describe the change that occurs in the bread and wine at Mass. Before the change, it is bread and wine. After the change, it looks like, smells like and tastes like bread and wine, but now it is something totally different."

In Father Turner's view, vocabulary is not a major problem. "People will readily understand the texts," he says. "The reason the missal includes such words is that the vocabulary in the Latin originals is so broad. Latin uses a variety of synonyms for words like 'sacrifice,' 'love,' 'mercy' and 'wonderful.' In order to represent that diversity and to provide variety among the prayers in English, a broad vocabulary is being used in the translation."

In recognition of the disturbance change can bring, he adds that bishops' conferences around the world have repeatedly stressed that these translations should not be used without prior and significant explanation. "One of the things we did not do 40 years ago, when the liturgy was first put into the vernacular, was to explain the changes fully," he says. "We need several layers of education and instruction about the translations, but even more importantly about the Mass itself."

The Liturgy Will Be More Formal, Theologically Deeper

Jerry Filteau

When a new English translation of the Mass is introduced in the United States—probably at the start of Advent in 2011—the style of worship will be more formal. But it will also be deeper theologically and more evocative emotionally and intellectually.

The Vatican's intention was not so much to make the liturgy more formal as to make the English version conform more closely to the original Latin, says Father Paul Turner, a Missouri priest who is former head of the North American Academy of Liturgy and frequently writes and lectures on liturgical questions.

"I think what's intentional is getting to a closer interpretation of the Latin" from which all modern liturgy translations in the Roman Catholic Church emanate, Father Turner says.

He said the result may sound more formal than in the past 40 years because the new translation rules inevitably lead in that direction.

The original translation of the *Roman Missal* into English was carried out under 1969 Vatican rules that stressed simplicity, modernity and other factors that would make the language of the liturgy more comprehensible and participatory.

Newer rules, set out by the Vatican in 2002, emphasize greater fidelity to the original Latin.

Msgr. John H. Burton, vicar general of the Diocese of Camden, N.J., and board chairman of the Federation of Diocesan Liturgical Coordinators, says there was concern "that the language has been too laid back" and failed to convey the rich liturgical heritage of the Roman rite.

The new translation shows an effort "to heighten the language a bit" and capture "the transcendence as well as the imminence of God," he says.

Father Andrew R. Wadsworth, executive director of the International Commission on English in the Liturgy, says a more formal language in the new translation "is clearly identifiable as one of its characteristics." The commission translates Latin liturgy texts into English for the world's English-speaking bishops' conferences.

He says the vocabulary of the Mass prayers "is necessarily rich as it reflects the various mysteries of salvation, conveying concepts which do not always occur in everyday conversation. To radically simplify the language is often to dilute the concept."

An excerpt from Eucharistic Prayer 1 illustrates the difference in style.

The version currently in use reads: "Look with favor on these offerings and accept them as once you accepted the gifts of your servant Abel, the sacrifice of Abraham, our father in faith, and the bread and wine offered by your priest Melchizedek.

"Almighty God, we pray that your angel may take this sacrifice to your altar in heaven. Then, as we receive from this altar the sacred body and blood of your Son, let us be filled with every grace and blessing."

The new translation says: "Be pleased to look upon these offerings with a serene and kindly countenance, and to accept them, as you were pleased to accept the gifts of your servant Abel the just, the sacrifice of Abraham, our father in faith, and the offering of your high priest Melchizedek, a holy sacrifice, a spotless victim.

"In humble prayer we ask you, almighty God: command that these gifts be borne by the hands of your holy angel to your altar on high in the sight of your divine majesty, so that all of us who through this participation at the altar receive the most holy body and blood of your Son may be filled with every grace and heavenly blessing."

In working to reflect features of the original Latin texts more clearly, the translators sought to develop "a translation which is clearly sacral in character and yet not archaic in style," Father Wadsworth says.

Father Turner says that one of the principles the first translators used was "compression," eliminating repetitive phrasing. "That lent a vigor to the first translation, but it did eliminate some of the style and content of the original prayers."

He acknowledges criticisms of some of the long, complex sentences in the new translation, especially in the collects, the prayers at the beginning of Mass.

"It's a logical fear that people will raise, but I think they'll be pleasantly surprised at how easy it is to understand." He says the collects follow a pattern, with many of the same components repeated from one day to the next. If you look at just one collect in the new translation, "it sounds complicated," he says. "But when you hear that style Sunday after Sunday, I think your ears open up to the style," and it becomes familiar.

Key Changes to the Missal Capture the Original Meanings

James Breig

Casual observers of the Roman Catholic Church often remark that it hasn't changed in 2,000 years. Actually, just like any living institution, it is constantly changing. Over the centuries, where and when the Mass is celebrated, how saints are chosen, and the method of electing popes are some of the ways the church has adjusted its traditions and policies.

Now come changes to the *Roman Missal,* the book containing the prayers for the Mass. For years, the church has been working to more accurately translate those prayers from the Latin in which the original missal is promulgated into modern languages, including English. Msgr. Kevin Irwin, dean of the School of Theology and Religious Studies at The Catholic University of America in Washington, says those alterations were necessitated by two factors.

"First, the committee charged with the English translation of the *Roman Missal* issued the post-Vatican II translations very quickly," he notes, referring to the Second Vatican Council in the 1960s. "They realized, after a few years' use of the missal, that some translations should have been more accurate. Second, some feasts have been added to the church's liturgical calendar in recent years, for example, St. Padre Pio's. Those Latin Masses need to be translated into English."

Peter Finn, associate director of the International Commission on English in the Liturgy (ICEL), compares the changes "to the cleaning of an old painting whose images are brought to clearer light in the cleaning process. . . . The translations have sought to achieve a suitable balance between the word-for-word, literal meaning of the Latin and the demands of good proclamation, style and intelligibility."

One of the most significant changes, Msgr. Irwin says, involves the familiar phrase, "And also with you," which the congregation recites after the celebrant of the Mass says, "The Lord be with you."

He explains that "the congregation will now say, 'and with your spirit.' This places the English translation in line with most other languages. The response is not to the person of the priest but to the Spirit of God, who ordained him to permanent service in the church. It is an acknowledgment of the 'spirit' and grace which is in him."

Msgr. Anthony Sherman, executive director of the U.S. bishops' Secretariat of Divine Worship, offers another example: Instead of saying "we believe" at the beginning of the creed, Catholics will soon recite, "I believe." The reason for the shift, he says, is "to underline the fact that, although we share our belief together with our brothers and sisters, each one of us is called to make an individual profession of faith."

As the changes are introduced, parishioners will have many guides to help them learn their new responses. "Plans are underway by a number of publishers to print up Mass booklets or cards containing the changes," Msgr. Irwin notes. Adds Msgr. Sherman: "Eventually all participation aids and hymnals will include the new responses of the people." Finn notes that "today, the people's responses can be made more readily available not only in printed editions but also on Web sites, CDs, iPhones, etc."

One Web site already available to help people become familiar with the new translation of the *Roman Missal* is sponsored by the U.S. Bishops: *www.usccb.org/romanmissal.*

Average Catholics may not immediately grasp the necessity and benefits of the changes, Msgr. Irwin admits, but the familiarity that comes with time should lead people to comfort with and understanding of the words.

"All of us—laity, clergy and religious—will need to take time to review the changed words and come to appreciate what we may not have understood or appreciated before," he says. "There are layers of meaning to liturgical texts, not just one meaning. These translations and the education we shall receive before they are implemented will offer us a chance to 'brush up' our knowledge of the Mass and of our beliefs."

Msgr. Sherman believes the changes "will invite the faithful to pause and reflect on what, after so many years, we may have taken for granted. People will listen more attentively to the various prayers proclaimed by the priest and these will convey a much deeper richness, which can be the basis for meditation and prayer for the enrichment of one's spiritual life."

Church Ministers Will Play a Crucial Role in Implementing the New Translation

Kate Blain

Now that the U.S. bishops and the Vatican have approved new English translations of the *Roman Missal,* the book of prayers used at Mass, experts say the next step is educating church ministers—from lectors to musicians—to better serve at liturgies.

Father Richard Hilgartner, associate director of the U.S. Conference of Catholic Bishops' Secretariat of Divine Worship, says the new adaptations of the missal will offer laypeople an opportunity to explore the great spiritual richness that can be found in these prayers.

"Just as priests who preside will have to prepare their proclamation of the prayers since the style is different from what is now prayed," he says, "the laity will experience some immediate changes in the responses they say at Mass."

For example, when the priest says, "The Lord be with you," the old response was, "And also with you." Now the people will respond, "And with your spirit."

Since church ministers serve at liturgies, says Father Hilgartner, they will be responsible in part for guiding the people in the pews to understand and adapt to these changes. To prepare for this, he says, lay ministers should "reflect on the new translation for their own spiritual growth and development."

He suggests that church ministers refer to the new texts during meetings at parishes and even open meetings by reciting some of the prayers from the new translation to become more comfortable with them and "gain access to the richness they contain." Doing so during special liturgical seasons like Advent and Lent, he adds, may smooth the transition further.

To prepare for the changes, the USCCB provides a new Web page (*www.usccb.org/romanmissal*) and is sponsoring a series of regional workshops for priests and parish leaders. The Federation of Diocesan Liturgical Commissions is planning workshops that can be given at parishes. Materials also are being published that can aid in adjusting to the liturgical changes.

Not all parish ministers will be affected by the changes. The translation of Scripture readings used at Mass will remain the same, so lectors will be unaffected. So will eucharistic ministers.

Church musicians, however, are another story. The changes to the *Roman Missal* will affect their ministry "pretty profoundly," says Michael McMahon, president of the National Association of Pastoral Musicians and a church music director.

Father Hilgartner explains, "Musicians will be challenged to lead the people in sung text that corresponds to the new translation. Composers have readjusted previous musical settings. New compositions are also being prepared that will broaden the treasury of music for the people."

McMahon says people can expect "new settings of many of the Mass texts that people have come to know and sing pretty confidently—the 'Gloria,' the 'Sanctus.' A lot of musical settings are being retooled."

While he doesn't expect the entire musical repertoire of most parishes to change, he says, one significant difference is that the new missal translation will "open up singing parts of the Mass we're not used to."

For example, he calls it a "priority in the new translation" to sing the dialogue at the beginning of the eucharistic prayer. He notes that singing more parts of the Mass "puts us at the same tempo," adding to the common experience of Mass-goers. McMahon sees the changes as a benefit since any part of the Mass given greater attention can result in greater understanding of the Mass by the people.

"People always need to be taken back to the basics of liturgical formation," he says, and the Second Vatican Council in the 1960s "called for full, active participation in the liturgy."

McMahon cautions that, despite the fact that change is coming, "we don't want to make too much or too little of it. We're not changing the Mass; we're changing the translation."

The Eucharistic Prayer: Our Response to God's Invitation

Lisa Maxson

What congregations say and hear at Mass will change with the new English translation of the *Roman Missal,* but the meaning of what one Catholic theologian calls the greatest prayer of the church is unchanged.

The eucharistic prayer, heard in the middle of every liturgy around the world, recalls the saving mystery of Jesus' death and resurrection and is the highest point of every Mass, says Msgr. Joseph DeGrocco, professor of liturgy and director of liturgical formation at Immaculate Conception Seminary in Huntington, N.Y.

The new translation does not change what's happening during the Mass, especially during the consecration, he says. It just brings the words said closer to the literal Latin translation.

"We believe that when the church prays the eucharistic prayer, that mystery is actually made present," Msgr. DeGrocco says. "Within that prayer, as part of that making present the mystery, the bread and wine are transformed into the body and blood of Christ."

Various forms of the eucharistic prayer will continue to be used throughout the year, depending on liturgical seasons and special occasions, Msgr. DeGrocco says. Each form expresses the essential beliefs of the Catholic Church, but emphasizes different aspects of the theology, he says.

Eucharistic prayer forms exist for Masses of reconciliation, Masses for various needs and occasions, regular Sunday Masses, and Masses with children.

Essentially the priest is free to choose whichever prayer he wants to use, but there are guidelines and aspects of good liturgical practice and theology that make some prayers more appropriate at times than others.

Each of the expressions of eucharistic prayer offers an emphasis, says Eileen Burke-Sullivan, S.T.D., assistant professor of Pastoral and Systematic Theology and director of the Master of Arts in Ministry Program at Creighton University in Omaha.

The reconciliation canons are usually prayed during Lent or during other times of public repentance or calls to repentance and forgiveness, she says.

The canons of various needs and occasions can be prayed when a group is gathered for a particular purpose, such as an assembly of school teachers, or a eucharistic congress, or a convention of musicians. While the assembly is probably not a regular Sunday congregation, it would be appropriate to pray one of the versions of this canon at a eucharistic celebration that, for example, missions the parish council or liturgical ministers, Burke-Sullivan says.

In 1973, eucharistic prayers for Masses with children were added to offer a simplified version of the eucharistic prayer to help children better understand the mystery and be engaged in the prayer, says Father Peter Mitchell, a professor of liturgy at St. Gregory the Great Seminary in Seward, Neb. These prayers were reserved for liturgies where young children were the primary assembly.

Many, however, criticized that by simplifying the text, the eucharistic prayer failed to convey an adequate sense of the sacred in the liturgy, Father Mitchell says, and so it was removed from the 2008 edition of the *Roman Missal.*

The eucharistic prayer is the body of Christ's response to the invitation it receives from God through the Word, Burke-Sullivan says.

"The response is always gratitude and it is always transformative," she says, but no words can possibly say it all.

By listening to the different eucharistic prayers throughout the year, people gain a better understanding of the beliefs of the Catholic Church.

"The way the prayers are written gives a sense of why and when they help the assembly to understand more fully how it is called to act more fully in the person of Christ," she says.

Msgr. DeGrocco agrees.

"The greater number of texts allows us to explore and enter in to the mystery of Christ in all its richness and various facets in a deeper way."

The eucharistic prayer is the prayer of thanksgiving and sanctification that takes place at the center of the Mass. During the prayer, one hears an account of Jesus' actions and his words at the Last Supper and the bread and wine become the body and blood of Christ.

The eucharistic prayer takes place after the Liturgy of the Word and the offertory and is introduced by a preface. The congregation kneels or stands during the eucharistic prayer, which ends at the singing of the Great Amen.

New Kids on the Block

Mary Elizabeth Sperry

When parishes start using the third edition of the *Roman Missal,* the texts of the prayers won't be the only changes Catholics in the pews see. The new missal will include 17 additions to the Proper of Saints, the part of the missal that includes prayers for the observances of saints' days. The Proper of Saints follows a calendar established by the Vatican and modified by the bishops of each country to include saints of local importance. Any changes to a national or diocesan calendar require the consent of the Vatican.

The saints new to the third edition of the *Roman Missal* include saints, like St. Augustine Zhao Rong, who were canonized after the second edition of the *Roman Missal* was published in 1985. Some of these saints, including St. Lawrence Ruiz and St. Andrew Dung-Lac, have been on the U.S. calendar for years. However, the new missal will be the first time their prayer texts have been available in the printed book. Other added saints appeared on the liturgical calendar until 1969, when the calendar was simplified and many saints' observances were removed. Also restored to the calendar are observances for the Most Holy Name of Jesus and the Most Holy Name of Mary. Still others saints and observances added to the missal highlight important teachings of the church such as the teaching on Mary (Our Lady of Fatima) and on the Eucharist as the sacrament of Christ's love (as promoted by St. Peter Julian Eymard).

By canonizing these holy men and women, the church presents them as models of Christian living. The added saints come from all eras and areas of the church's life—from the fourth century (St. Catherine of Alexandria and St. Apollinaris) to the 20th century (St. Josephine Bakhita, St. Christopher Magallenes and St. Pio of Pietrelcina)—and from Europe, Africa, Asia and the Americas. They include priests, religious women, martyrs, a married woman and missionaries.

Whether or not Catholics hear about these saints at their local parishes will depend on the priest. With the exception of the memorials of St. Teresa Benedicta of the Cross (better known as Edith Stein) and St. Pio of Pietrelcina (better known as Padre Pio), all of the new observances are optional memorials. That means the decision about whether or not to celebrate them at a particular Mass rests with the celebrating priest. While a priest may not add the observance of a saint or blessed not on the approved calendar, he is free to decide which, if any, optional memorials he will celebrate. In choosing among the possible observances, priests might highlight saints who offer a particular example to their people.

These new additions are not the final word about saints on the calendar. The church will continue to canonize new saints as models for the faithful. Some of these saints will be celebrated in those parts of the world where they served. Others will be placed on the general calendar, celebrated by the Universal Church to unite the liturgy of heaven with that of earth.

NEW SAINTS AND OBSERVANCES IN THE THIRD EDITION OF THE *ROMAN MISSAL*

✠ **January 3: Most Holy Name of Jesus.** This is part of the church's celebration of Christmas, recognizing that God "bestowed on [Jesus] the name that is above every name" (Philippians 2:9).

✠ **February 8: St. Josephine Bakhita, virgin.** Born in Darfur, Josephine survived kidnapping and slavery to become a nun who embraced and lived hope as a redeemed child of God.

✠ **April 23: St. Adalbert, bishop and martyr.** Martyred near the end of the first millennium, Adalbert was a missionary in the countries of central Europe, striving to bring unity to God's people.

✠ **April 28: St. Louis Mary de Montfort, priest.** This French priest is best known for his devotion to Mary, encouraging the faithful to approach Jesus through his mother.

✠ **May 13: Our Lady of Fatima.** The Virgin Mary appeared to three children in the Portuguese town of Fatima in 1917. During these apparitions, she encouraged penance and praying the rosary.

✠ **May 21: Sts. Christopher Magallanes, priest and martyr, & Companions, martyrs.** Martyred in 1927, this Mexican priest was noted for his care of the native peoples of Mexico and for his work to support vocations to the priesthood.

✠ **May 22: St. Rita of Cascia, religious.** A wife, mother, widow and nun, St. Rita was known for her patience and humility in spite of many hardships. Conforming herself to the crucified Christ, she bore a wound on her forehead similar to one inflicted by a crown of thorns.

✠ **July 9: Sts. Augustine Zhao Rong, priest and martyr, & Companions, martyrs.** Canonized with 119 other Chinese martyrs, Augustine began his career as a soldier. Inspired by the martyrs, he was baptized and eventually became a priest and martyr himself.

✠ **July 20: St. Apollinaris, bishop and martyr.** Martyred in the second century, Apollinarius was the Bishop of Ravenna in Italy. He was known as a great preacher and miracle worker.

✠ **July 24: St. Sharbel Makhluf, priest.** A Maronite priest in Lebanon, St. Sharbel spent much of his life as a hermit in the desert, living a life of extreme penance.

✠ **August 2: St. Peter Julian Eymard, priest.** Founder of the Congregation of the Blessed Sacrament, St. Peter devoted his life to promoting first Communions and devotion to the Eucharist as the sacrament of Christ's love.

✠ **August 9: St. Teresa Benedicta of the Cross, virgin and martyr.** Born of Jewish parents as Edith Stein, she received academic renown as a philosopher. After her conversion to Catholicism, she became a Carmelite nun. She died in Auschwitz in 1942.

✠ **September 12: Most Holy Name of Mary.** After beginning in Spain in 1513, this celebration became a universal feast in the 17th century. A companion to the Memorial of The Most Holy Name of Jesus, it follows the Feast of the Nativity of Mary.

✠ **September 23: St. Pio of Pietrelcina, priest.** Padre Pio was known throughout Italy and the world for his patient hearing of confessions and for his spiritual guidance. In poor health for much of his life, he conformed his sufferings to those of Christ.

✠ **September 28: Sts. Lawrence Ruiz & Companions, martyrs.**
St. Lawrence and his companions spread the Gospel in the Philippines, Taiwan, and Japan. St. Lawrence was born in Manila and was a husband and father.

✠ **November 24: Sts. Andrew Dũng-Lạc, priest and martyr, & Companions, martyrs.** St. Andrew and his 107 companions, both priests and laity, were martyred in Vietnam in the 17th through 19th centuries. Through their preaching, lives of faith, and witness unto death, they strengthened the church in Vietnam.

✠ **November 25: St. Catherine of Alexandria, virgin and martyr.** Martyred in the early part of the fourth century, Catherine was known for her intelligence, her deep faith, and the power of her intercession.

All Life Leads to, and from, the Mass

Terry McGuire

Ask a Catholic liturgist where Catholics find their identity, and the answer comes without hesitation: the Mass.

"It's where we are most 'church,' if you will; where we are most the body of Christ," says Msgr. John Burton, chair of the board of directors of the Federation of Diocesan Liturgical Commissions. "The Mass is at the very heart of our Christian experience."

For Precious Blood Sister Joyce Ann Zimmerman, director of the Institute for Liturgical Ministry in Dayton, Ohio, the Mass is far more than a Sunday obligation or even a mere ritual.

"We cannot be Roman Catholic without Mass," she says. "Mass actually defines for us who we are as baptized members of the body of Christ."

And that, the two liturgists say, is why the Mass is so important to Catholicism.

Sister Joyce Ann notes that the Mass is where Christ gives himself to us in word and sacrament, offering his "total self-giving love" that marks his divinity and humanity. "That total self-giving is what our life as baptized people is also all about," she says. At Mass, "we enter into and rehearse who we are to be and how we are to be as the visible presence of Christ in the world today."

Catholics' participation in the celebration of the Mass is a celebration of salvation, says Sister Janet Baxendale of the Sisters of Charity, a professor of liturgy at St. Joseph Seminary in Yonkers, N.Y.

"This is one of the primary reasons that the Mass is at the center of our life as Catholics," Sister Janet says. "The bread and wine offered on the altar truly become the body and blood of Christ which was sacrificed for our salvation. This eucharistic food nourishes us spiritually. It is our food for the journey of life."

The three liturgists note that upcoming changes to the English translation of the *Roman Missal* will likely cause concern among some because of the deeply personal way in which the Mass touches people.

Some tend to become very protective in the face of change, Sister Joyce Ann says. But the liturgy is a communal gathering and not an individual event. When a person comes through the church doors and enters the sacred space, they leave the individual self outside and join the gathering as members of the body of Christ, becoming "we" instead of "I," she says. The realization that the "liturgy isn't about me" should help people prepare for the changes, she says. They have to "let go" and place their trust that the Spirit and the teaching office of the church will be moving them forward.

The new changes are not being made for the sake of change but to be as "faithful as possible to the Latin texts from which they were translated," Sister Janet says. While they may take some getting used to, "they can be for us a way to grow in a deeper understanding of and appreciation for the power and beauty of the great treasure we have in our Mass."

The three liturgists note that the Mass, as the summit of all the church's services, differs from the other sacraments and popular devotions such as the rosary, Stations of the Cross, novenas and other forms of private prayer.

"Both private prayer and popular devotions are strongly encouraged by the church," Sister Janet says, but "while they are a help to our celebrating liturgy well—to putting us into the spirit of the liturgy—they are in no way equal to the liturgy."

Msgr. Burton likes to look at the Mass from a monastic perspective, where the Mass is at the center of the day and everything leads to it and flows from it.

As Catholics, all of life leads to the Mass, he says, and "all of life leads from it."

The Mass: Source of Strength for Daily Life

María de Lourdes Ruiz Scaperlanda

Catholics believe that in the celebration of the Mass, they join the sacrifice of everyday life to the sacrifice of Christ, says Msgr. Joseph DeGrocco, Professor of Liturgy at Immaculate Conception Seminary in Huntington, N.Y. "The offering and self-emptying we do at Mass, in union with Christ, is the offering and self-emptying we are supposed to be living every moment of every day—that is what the Christian life is!"

The relationship between the Mass and everyday life is a reciprocal relationship, an active experience. At every Mass Catholics bring the offering of what's going on in their lives—and offer that in union with Jesus. It is that union, culminating in the holy Communion, that strengthens them for everyday life, explains Msgr. DeGrocco. "We do liturgy in order to try to do Christian life right. What we do at Mass is a summation or a 'microcosm,' if you will, of the way we are supposed to be living Christian life."

According to Msgr. DeGrocco, this awareness of what takes place at every Mass is precisely why Catholics should invest themselves into appreciating the Mass. "We cannot be Catholic without it," he says. "We cannot be fully united to Jesus without sacramental communion with him in the Eucharist."

Not only is daily life about the Mass, says Liturgy Professor Sister Janet Baxendale, SC of New York City's St. Joseph's Seminary, but the Mass also "offers extraordinary help in my efforts to live my life well" through Scripture, the word of God, the prayers of the faithful, and most powerfully, by receiving the Eucharist.

In holy Communion, "Christ comes to us to nourish us; to be food for our souls as we struggle to fulfill our baptismal call to be like Christ, to be his presence in our world," notes Sister Janet.

Distractions can make participation and appreciation of the Mass discouraging, notes Sister Janet. "Our thoughts stray; we find ourselves trying to solve problems of home, of office, of life in general. The people around us distract us: a crying child; someone with an annoying habit sharing 'my' pew; the choir is off-key; the readings can't be heard—and on and on."

Sister Janet says there are strategies to reduce the impact of these distractions:

- Prepare for Mass. Read over that day's Scriptures. "In this way you will have done the 'ground work,' tilling the soil so that the seed of God's word may find ready soil in you."
- Participate in Mass. Sing the hymns, pray the responses, listen to the readings and to the prayers said by the priest on our behalf: the opening prayer, the prayer over the gifts, the prayer after Communion, the eucharistic prayer. "Work at doing this well, and there will be less time for distractions."
- Learn about the Mass. Check online sources provided by the U.S. Conference of Catholic Bishops and printed materials in your own parish for resources to "enhance your understanding and appreciation of the great gift God has given to his people in the Mass."
- Take daily time to be silent and to listen. The self-discipline of a regular period of quiet reflection teaches us to "empty our minds of the cares, ideas, and distracting thoughts that press on us—and to concentrate on God, on his incredible love for me [personally], and his presence to me. Our perseverance can bear fruit in the ability to concentrate more fully when we are at Mass."
- Don't get discouraged. "It is the effort that counts. The results are in the hands of God."

Christ is present at Mass in many ways, explains Msgr. DeGrocco, "in the gathered assembly, in the Word, in the priest, and most especially in the real presence of the Eucharist. . . . The person in the pew who does nothing 'more' than being internally attentive and bringing the sacrifice of his/her life, and who does all the external participation (sitting, standing, kneeling, responding, singing) is nonetheless participating fully."

He notes, "The best way to improve one's appreciation of the Mass is to improve one's living of the sacrifice of one's life."

About the Authors

Kate Blain is a freelance writer and managing editor of *The Evangelist*, newspaper of the Diocese of Albany, N.Y.

James Breig, a long-time diocesan newspaper editor and freelance writer, has written hundreds of articles for Catholic magazines. For 25 years, he also authored an award-winning column on the media for Catholic newspapers. Now retired, he continues to write and is working on a book about World War II.

Beth Dotson Brown is the author of *Yes! I Am Catholic*, contributes to a variety of Catholic publications and writes a blog about eating from the garden. You can reach her through her website at *www.bethdotsonbrown.net*.

Peter Feuerherd is a freelance writer, communications consultant for the NY Province of the Society of Jesus, and adjunct professor of journalism and communications at St. John's University, N.Y.

Jerry Filteau has covered liturgical issues in the Catholic press since 1973, first for Catholic News Service and, since his retirement there in 2007, for *National Catholic Reporter*.

Lisa Maxson is associate editor, writer and photographer at the *Catholic Voice*, the newspaper of the Archdiocese of Omaha, Neb.

Terry McGuire, Ed.D. is a specialist in the area of organizational mission and human development. He has published extensively in the area of mission and ministry, corporate culture, change management, and community networking.

María de Lourdes Ruiz Scaperlanda is a frequent contributor to the Catholic press. She is an award-winning journalist and the author of five books. See *www.mymaria.net*.

Mary Elizabeth Sperry holds a master's degree in liturgical studies from the Catholic University of America and is a frequent speaker on Scripture and the liturgy.

Lynn Williams is a full-time communications consultant and an award-winning freelance journalist from Nashville, Tenn. She is a frequent contributor to the Catholic press.